To Mom

Christmas 2007

Love Rob

THANK YOU FOR BEING
my mother

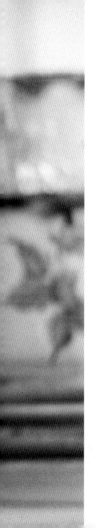

THANK YOU FOR BEING
my mother

Jacqui Ripley

RYLAND
PETERS
& SMALL
LONDON NEW YORK

Designer Pamela Daniels
Editor Annabel Morgan
Picture Researcher Emily Westlake
Production Gordana Simakovic
Art Director Anne-Marie Bulat
Publishing Director Alison Starling

First published in the United States
in 2007 by Ryland Peters & Small, Inc
519 Broadway, Fifth floor
New York, NY 10012
www.rylandpeters.com

10 9 8 7 6 5 4 3 2 1

Text © Jacqui Ripley 2007
Design and photographs
© Ryland Peters & Small 2007

ISBN: 978-1-84597-397-1

Printed in China

Contents

Introduction

Mothers are amazing. They are generous, loving, loyal, and fun. They nurture, teach, and mold us. We owe them everything, but often it's difficult to put the love and gratitude we feel for our mothers into words.

This little book has a big message—it aims to tell your mother how much you love and cherish her, as well as letting her know how significantly she has shaped your life and how grateful you are. Although every mother is different, many of the "thank yous" in this book will no doubt ring true for your mom, bringing a smile to her face and maybe even a tear to her eye.

From treasured childhood memories to the times when she gave you love, comfort, and understanding when it was most needed, to the words of wisdom she blessed you with and that you have carried with you into adulthood, this book says a huge and heartfelt thank you to one of the most special people in your life—your mother.

childhood

*Life began with waking up and
loving my mother's face.*

GEORGE ELIOT

Thank you for teaching me to appreciate the simple pleasures in life, such as sitting down to a family meal, or dancing to our favorite song when it came on the radio and singing along at the tops of our voices.

Thank you for taking my sister and me on all those happy summer vacations. Money was tight, but all we needed to keep us content was building sandcastles, running on the beach, and eating ice-cream, along with lots of fun, games, and laughter.

Thank you for always making my friends feel extra-special when they came over to hang out after school. I used to feel so proud that my mom had baked a cake especially for them!

Thank you for taking "my" dog for his daily walk for many years after I begged you to get him, having promised that I would dutifully exercise him every single day. Needless to say, my good intentions lasted for about a week…

Thank you for always miraculously knowing where everything was at a moment's notice, and for being such a great finder of lost socks, missing sneakers, and elusive schoolbooks!

Thank you for all those evenings you spent patiently helping me with my homework, and for confessing that math was never your strong point either. I always felt I had a secret ally.

Thank you for all the stories we shared. I remember you reading *Rapunzel* over and over again before bedtime. I never tired of hearing the line "Rapunzel, Rapunzel, let down your hair," but I'm sure you did—although you never showed it!

Thank you for being a soccer mom, a karate mom, and a swimming mom. I loved you for supporting all my sporting passions—however short-lived they were!

Thank you for being a cowboy, a pirate, a nurse, and an astronaut... in fact, anything I wanted you to be in our make-believe games.

Thank you for not telling the distant relatives we were staying with that I had wet the bed. You made up a story about having tripped and spilled a glass of water onto my mattress. I was so grateful to you for covering up for me that I could have kissed you!

Thank you for making Mother's Day my day too, by always giving me a little gift. You always said that, after all, if it wasn't for me you wouldn't be a mother.

Thank you for having the tact not to interrogate me about my very first proper kiss, even though I had stood on the doorstep with the kisser for over an hour one cold winter evening!

Thank you for always making me special party dresses. I remember the excitement of choosing the pattern and the fabric, then you would whizz up a beautiful creation on your trusty old sewing machine. Haute couture, eat your heart out!

Thank you for indulging all my childhood fantasies. I loved the way you used to walk through the forest with me looking for trees with hollows in the trunks. We would put little home-made gifts in for the tree fairies.

Thank you for wrapping me in aluminum foil from head to toe in honor of the fancy-dress day at school. I won first prize as the Tin Man from *The Wizard of Oz!*

manners

Politeness of the mind is to have
delicate thoughts.

FRANCOIS DE LA ROCHEFOUCAULD

Thank you for teaching me the valuable gift of listening. You always drummed it into us that we should never interrupt halfway through somebody's sentence. It was a worthwhile lesson— from really listening to people, I've gained far more insight into what they truly have to say.

Thank you for telling me that there's never any excuse not to respond to an invitation.

Thank you for making such a fuss about our table manners. Yes, I know I used to roll my eyes and heave a sigh when you told us to sit up straight and hold our forks properly, but now I know that good manners are all about showing other people the respect that is due to them.

Thank you for bringing me up to always say "please" and "thank you," whatever the situation. They are such small words but, as I have found to my advantage, get such a big response.

Thank you for being such a wonderful role model. You taught me by example to be kind-hearted, considerate, and a loyal friend.

Thank you for telling me it's not stylish to be late for dates—just downright rude!

Thank you for teaching me to accept a compliment just as I would a gift—with pleasure, rather than embarrassment.

Thank you for telling me that, in a man, good manners are far more important than movie-star good looks. Women like being treated like a woman, not like one of the guys.

Thank you for teaching me that respect for others costs nothing, but is worth its weight in gold.

Thank you for showing me by example that we should always ask politely, rather than making demands. It's got me so much further in life.

Thank you for explaining that, sometimes when people seem rude or abrupt they're just shy. If people aren't forthcoming in a conversation, instead of thinking they're unfriendly, I always give them the benefit of the doubt.

Thank you for telling me always to be polite to waiters. I cringe when I eat with people who barely give them a second glance, let alone say "thank you." Good manners cost nothing, but they make the world a much pleasanter place.

Thank you for teaching me that even a pre-packed sandwich or a supermarket ready-meal tastes better when it's eaten from a china plate.

Thank you for forcing us to sit down and write thank-you notes to anyone who gave us a gift. It's become an ingrained habit, and I know that a written "thank you" gives so much more satisfaction than an e-mail, sms message, or telephone call.

Thank you for telling me that a really good friend is someone who discreetly whispers that you have lipstick on your teeth or a smudge on your nose.

Thank you for teaching my brother and I the "golden rule": that we should always treat others the way we want to be treated ourselves. That rule is still absolutely fundamental to my life today.

comfort

Shared joys are a double joy,
shared sorrow is half a sorrow.

SWEDISH PROVERB

Thank you for making special days special. I always had the biggest pumpkin at Halloween, the loudest fireworks on Independence Day, an overly decorated tree at Christmas (who cared if it didn't look stylish!), and a mouth-watering homemade cake on my birthday.

Thank you for making rainy summer days less depressing by throwing an impromptu movie screening. We'd all snuggle on the sofa, eat pizza and popcorn, and slurp shakes.

Thank you for taking yourself out, along with my (reluctant) dad, so I could enjoy my 18th birthday party at home without my parents cramping my style. And thank you for not going totally crazy after you found your favorite pot plant had been decapitated!

Thank you for our regular Sunday morning "bed bug" sessions. I loved those moments cuddled down under the comforter together with a favorite book.

Thank you for pampering me with hot milk, hot soup, and, most importantly, a hot-water bottle—all brought to me in bed whenever I was sick. It always made me feel much better.

Thank you for inventing the cuddle couch. Whenever I felt down or near to tears, out would come the blanket, you would beckon me over to the cuddle couch, wrap me up, and give me a big, comforting bear hug. That always gave me strength enough to dry my tears.

Thank you for making bath times such fun. I remember you warming the hugest, fluffiest towel in the dryer, wrapping me tightly in it, and then singing kooky made-up songs as you rubbed me dry.

Thank you for being a shoulder to weep on after my first great love (I was 12!) left me for another girl. You knew a shopping trip to buy a new pair of jeans and a top was all I needed to get over him.

Thank you for doing all those "mom" things that I was too young to appreciate at the time—clean and ironed clothes, home-cooked meals, and a smile and a hug when I arrived home from school.

Thank you for your mother's intuition. You always knew when something was wrong, even if I didn't tell you.

Thank you for making me feel pretty and grown up even at a young age. Every Saturday you allowed me to put on my best dress and we would have a milkshake at the ice-cream parlor. I felt like a princess!

Thank you for putting little notes in my lunchbox. You used to write things like "Cheese makes strong and happy bones" and "Carrots make your eyes sparkle." I used to look forward to reading them every day!

Thank you for being such a great grandmother. When I can't be around, I can relax when I know my son is being looked after by you.

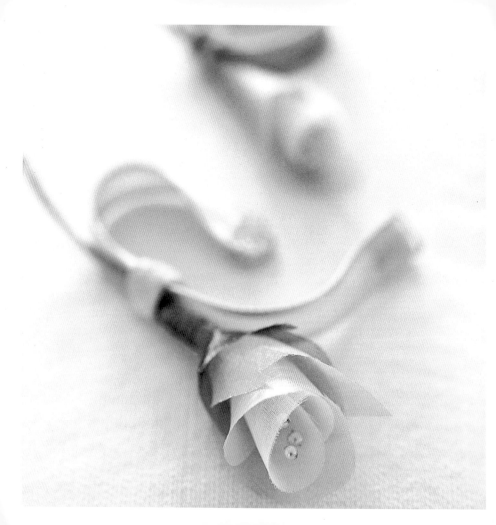

wisdom

*To know when to be generous and
when firm—that is wisdom.*

ELBERT HUBBARD

Thank you for telling me that giving up doesn't mean I'm weak. You always said that sometimes you have to be strong enough to let go. You don't know how much those words have rung true during my life.

Thank you for encouraging me to live outside my means. Not in the financial sense, but by pushing me not to play it safe when I needed to move outside my comfort zone. As a mother, that was quite unconventional, and I loved you for it.

Thank you for for always reminding me that I have choices. If I'm not happy with one, you always told me to choose another.

Thank you for always encouraging me to take an interest in life. Books, movies, newspapers, and the theater featured heavily in my upbringing. "If you're interested, you'll be interesting," you always said.

Thank you for talking me out of having a tattoo when I was a teenager. Your wry observation was that art should be saved for the canvas, not etched on the body.

Thank you for telling me a gift
isn't given with thought and love if it
hasn't been wrapped properly. For me,
the gift-wrapping is half the fun of
giving a present.

Thank you for telling me that old friendships can be as cozy as an old pair of slippers, but that I should try and make my marriage feel like an expensive pair of heels.

Thank you for teaching me never to be afraid to ask questions... or directions!

Thank you for helping me realize that if a boyfriend says he doesn't deserve me, then he probably doesn't. And if he says I'm too good for him, then I probably am!

Thank you for telling me never to let a man put me off my food or make me feel bad about my thighs!

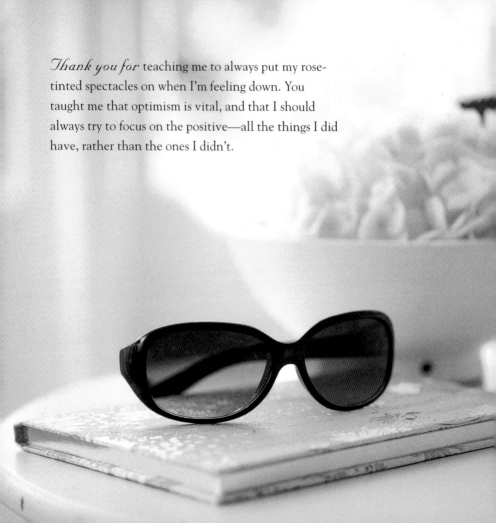

Thank you for teaching me to always put my rose-tinted spectacles on when I'm feeling down. You taught me that optimism is vital, and that I should always try to focus on the positive—all the things I did have, rather than the ones I didn't.

Thank you for telling me the word "sorry"
can be the hardest thing to say, but the most
comforting thing to hear.

beauty

Though we travel the world over to find the beautiful, we must carry it with us or we find it not.

RALPH WALDO EMERSON

Thank you for always slathering me in sunblock lotion, even thought I hated it and it was during a time when being pale wasn't fashionable. My skin has never stopped thanking you to this day.

Thank you for encouraging me to notice the beauty all around me from an early age—from the prettiest of flowers to the tallest of trees.

Thank you for making me wear braces—even if it did take a few bribes. My tears were relentless at first, as I viewed my crooked teeth through metal bars. But now, decades later, people often compliment me on my straight, white smile.

Thank you for always making me feel like a star and bolstering my self-esteem. Even through my grumpy teenage years, when I used to say I hated myself, you would always say I was beautiful in your eyes, as well as many others.

Thank you for sending me to ballet classes. There's no better beauty tip in the world than good posture and poise.

Thank you for showing me that properly applied make-up could turn even the humblest daisy into a blossoming rose.

Thank you for buying me endless supplies of acne cream and concealer during my adolescent years, when my hormones were raging. You always understood when I felt low about my skin and tried your hardest to make my complexion better behaved.

Thank you for giving me crazy manicures where you used to paint every nail a different color. And thank you for letting me give you a manicure where I used to paint every nail really badly!

Thank you for hiding the tweezers when I got rather carried away plucking my eyebrows!

Thank you for buying me my first bra.
Yes, my chest was as flat as a pancake, but
you took me seriously and understood my
need to feel sophisticated when we shopped
together for the smallest but prettiest one.

Thank you for introducing me to dressing-table beauty. I always remember the way you applied your lipstick before an evening out, the ritual lengthening of your lashes with black mascara, and the starlet way you used to apply your perfume behind your ears and on your wrists with the bottle stopper.

Thank you for believing in the importance of a good haircut. At school, my hair was the envy of all those little girls who had to suffer the indignity of a pudding-basin-style home hair cut! I always felt my hair was my crowning glory, thanks to its professional styling.

Thank you for teaching me that a woman should never go anywhere or make any vital decision without wearing a swipe of lipstick.

picture credits

Key: ph= photographer, a=above, b=below,
r=right, l=left, c=center.

Page 1 ph Polly Wreford; 2 ph Debi
Treloar/ceramicist Jette Arendal Winther's
home in Denmark (www.arendal-ceramics.com);
4 & 5 ph Polly Wreford; 6 ph Chris
Tubbs/Giorgio and Ilaria Miani's Podere Buon
Riposo in Val d'Orcia (ilariamiani@tin.it); 8 ph
Winfred Heinze; 10 & 11 ph William
Lingwood; 12 & 13 ph Caroline Arber/item
designed and made by Jane Cassini and Ann
Brownfield (jane_vintagestyle@yahoo.com);
14 & 15a ph Winfred Heinze; 15b ph Polly
Wreford; 16-17 ph Winfred Heinze; 18-19 ph
Claire Richardson; 20 ph Chris Tubbs/artist
Camilla d'Afflitto's home in Tuscany
(055 64 99 237/222); 22-23 ph Polly Wreford;
24 ph Caroline Arber/designed and made by
Jane Cassini and Ann Brownfield; 25 ph
Catherine Gratwicke/Martin Barrell and
Amanda Sellers' apartment, owners of
Maisonette (www.maisonette.uk.com); 26-31
ph Caroline Arber/designed and made by Jane
Cassini and Ann Brownfield; 32 ph Debi
Treloar/Christina and Allan Thaulow's home in
Denmark; 34 ph Polly Wreford; 36-37 ph Debi
Treloar/designer Petra Boase and family's home
in Norfolk (www.petraboase.com); 38 ph
Winfred Heinze; 39 ph Debi Treloar; 40 ph
Claire Richardson; 41 ph Debi Treloar; 42-45
ph Caroline Arber/designed and made by Jane
Cassini and Ann Brownfield; 46a ph Debi
Treloar; 46b ph Catherine Gratwicke; 47 &
48a ph Polly Wreford; 48b ph Claire
Richardson; 49 ph Sandra Lane; 50 ph Winfred
Heinze; 51 ph Caroline Arber/designed and
made by Jane Cassini and Ann Brownfield;
52 ph Winfred Heinze; 55-57 ph Claire
Richardson; 58 ph Winfred Heinze; 59-61 ph
Claire Richardson; 62 ph Simon Upton; 64 &
endpapers ph Debi Treloar/ceramicist Jette
Arendal Winther's home in Denmark.

acknowledgments

Thank you to the many friends who passed on their personal memories about their own mothers to me, and thank you to my own mother, Hazel.